PATIENCE

Patience

EDITED BY LIN SEXTON

Ariel Books

Andrews and McMeel

Kansas City

ISBN: 0-8362-3119-8

Library of Congress Catalog Card Number: 95-60376

INTRODUCTION

*P*ATIENCE is not simply a virtue: it is an unfolding of life. It is also an enhancing, an enriching, of that life. Rush to meet a goal, and you may achieve it; but if you walk toward it slowly, attentively—with patience— then you will have both the ultimate joy of reaching your goal and the excitement of the journey itself.

Patience may seem an old-fashioned and out-of-date virtue in our ceaselessly hectic age, but in fact it is brimming with humanity. Patience demands that we smell the rose, not merely admire it, that we lay the solid foundation of a house, not merely throw together a few bricks and some mortar. The man or woman who rushes through life merely exists. The man or woman who tastes, feels, smells, *senses* that life—who has the patience to taste, feel, smell, sense that life—is the one who truly lives.

Begin with patience,
end with pleasure.
—AFRICAN PROVERB

The world belongs
to the patient man.
—ITALIAN PROVERB

The drops of rain make a
hole in the stone not by
violence but by oft falling.

—LUCRETIUS

$\mathcal{B}$E patient. How often we have admonished ourselves and others to practice patience. But how do we learn patience? Perhaps the first step is to recognize the symptoms of impatience when they arise: restlessness, worry, nervousness, tension. Recognition can be a powerful tool for change. In some instances, it may be all that's needed to set the wheels of patience in motion.

Patience, and the mulberry
leaf, becomes a silk gown.
—CHINESE PROVERB

The strongest of all warriors are
these two—Time and Patience.
—LEO TOLSTOY

The hill hath not yet raised its head
to heaven that perseverance cannot
gain the summit of in time.
—CHARLES DICKENS

THE WORLD IS AGAINST ME

"The world is against me,"
   he said with a sigh,
"Somebody stops every scheme
   that I try.
The world has me down and
   it's keeping me there;
I don't get a chance. Oh,
   the world is unfair!
When a fellow is poor then
   he can't get a show;
The world is determined to
   keep him down low."

"What of Abe Lincoln?" I
    asked. "Would you say
That he was much richer than
    you are to-day?
He hadn't your chance of
    making his mark,
And his outlook was often
    exceedingly dark;
Yet he clung to his purpose with
    courage most grim
And he got to the top. Was the
    world against him?"

"I could name you a dozen, yes,
  hundreds, I guess,
Of poor boys who've patiently
  climbed to success;
All boys who were down and
  who struggled alone,
Who'd have thought themselves
  rich if your fortune they'd known;
Yet they rose in the world you're
  so quick to condemn,
And I'm asking you now, was the
  world against them?"

—EDGAR A. GUEST

14

The remedy against bad times is
to have patience with them.

—ARAB PROVERB

Patience is a necessary
ingredient of genius.
—BENJAMIN DISRAELI

$\mathcal{E}$VERYTHING unfolds at its own pace, no matter how hard we push it. Learn to let things take their natural course, and you will find that patience follows.

There is no joy but calm.

—ALFRED, LORD TENNYSON

Genius is nothing but a
greater aptitude for patience.
—GEORGE LOUIS
LECLERC DE BUFFON

Upon the heat and flame
of thy distemper
Sprinkle cool patience.

—WILLIAM SHAKESPEARE

ONE path to patience is learning to pay attention. When we are totally engaged in what we are doing, we are freed from the tensions associated with impatience. We simply live our lives from moment to moment, meeting each new situation as it arises with calm equanimity.

The salt of patience
seasons everything.
—ITALIAN PROVERB

Patience is sorrow's salve.
—CHARLES CHURCHILL

Keep cool: it will be all
one a hundred years hence.
—RALPH WALDO EMERSON

The greatest prayer is patience.

—GAUTAMA BUDDHA

Patience is the best remedy
for every trouble.

—TITUS MACCIUS PLAUTUS

Sit and wait for the
good chestnuts.

—SAMOAN PROVERB

$\mathscr{W}$E look for many qualities in a true friend, and patience is always one of them. A patient friend is ready to listen, slow to criticize, quick to sympathize, and equally quick to understand. Strive to carry stores of patience and kindness wherever you go. See what happens. Situations that previously appeared intimidating or hostile may suddenly become friendly and inviting. Be patient. Who knows what might develop.

He who is slow to anger is
better than the mighty,
and he who rules his spirit
than he who takes a city.

—Proverbs 16:32

Never think that God's delays are
God's denials. Hold on; hold fast;
hold out. Patience is genius.

—COMTE DE BUFFON

Sir Henry Wotton . . . was a most
dear lover, and a frequent practicer
of the art of angling; of which he
would say, "it was an employment
for his idle time, which was
then not idly spent . . . a rest to his
mind, a cheerer of his spirits, a
diverter of sadness, a calmer of
unquiet thoughts, a moderator
of passions, a procurer of
contentedness; and that it begat
habits of peace and patience in those
that professed and practiced it."

—IZAAK WALTON

Sorrow and silence are strong, and
patient endurance is godlike.
—HENRY WADSWORTH
LONGFELLOW

When angry, count four;
when very angry, swear.

—MARK TWAIN

REPRIMAND a child in public, his anger and humiliation will block out any lesson you are trying to teach. Choose patience instead: protect your child's dignity, and scold or correct him in private. Your choice will be rewarded when you see that he has taken your lesson to heart, and without resentment.

They also serve who
only stand and wait.
—JOHN MILTON

Speak when you are angry
and you will make the best
speech you will ever regret.
—AMBROSE BIERCE

There are no short cuts to
Heaven, only the ordinary
way of ordinary things.
—VINCENT MCNABB

To accept what you are is to be
content, and contentment is the
greatest wealth. To work with
patience is to gather power. To
surrender to the Eternal flow
is to be completely present.

—VIMALA MCCLURE

*M*OST aspects of our lives are regulated by calendars and clocks. The natural flow of time and events seems completely incompatible with our modern lifestyles. Patience, however, reveals that these arbitrary blocks of time are just that—arbitrary. Though appointments and schedules will always be part of our lives, whenever possible we should allow ourselves to move to the beat of our own internal rhythms. By doing so, we become acquainted with the inherent qualities of patience: calm, composure, and peace. And the more familiar we become with these qualities, the more eager we may become to integrate them into our daily affairs.

Patience is a good nag,
but she'll bolt.

—ENGLISH PROVERB

Who hangs on, wins.

—PENNSYLVANIA GERMAN PROVERB

The Rainy Day

The day is cold, and dark, and dreary;
It rains, and the wind is never weary;
The vine still clings to the mouldering
    wall,
But at every gust the dead leaves fall,
    And the day is dark and dreary.

My life is cold, and dark, and dreary;
It rains, and the wind is never weary;
My thoughts still cling to the
    mouldering past,

But the hopes of youth fall thick
    in the blast,
    And the days are dark and dreary.

Be still, sad heart! and cease repining;
Behind the clouds is the sun still
    shining;
Thy fate is the common fate of all,
Into each life some rain must fall,
    Some days must be dark and dreary.
      —HENRY WADSWORTH
        LONGFELLOW

Patience is the best of dispositions: he who possesses patience, possesses all things.

—AFRICAN PROVERB

WHEN the reward is in sight, patience comes easily. When the reward is distant, uncertain, or ambiguous, then patience becomes more difficult. That is when we need it most of all; and that is the kind of patience that will see us through all of the vicissitudes of life.

The person who makes a success
of living is the one who sees his
goal steadily and aims for it
unswervingly. That is dedication.

—CECIL B. DE MILLE

Have patience with all things,
but chiefly have patience with
yourself. Do not lose courage
in considering your own
imperfections, but instantly set
about remedying them—every
day begin the task anew.

—St. Francis de Sales

Our greatest glory is not
in never falling, but in
rising every time we fall.
—OLIVER GOLDSMITH

How poor are they that
have not patience!
What wound did ever heal
but by degrees?

—WILLIAM SHAKESPEARE

Delay is preferable to error.

—THOMAS JEFFERSON

*A*PPROACH each task as if it were a bottle of wine aging in a cool cellar. Rush to drink it and all will be lost: the taste, the bouquet, the color. Be patient and you'll get a fine wine: subtle, complex, and long lasting. Refuse to be hurried, and refuse to hurry others.

Patience is safety, haste is blame.

—TURKISH PROVERB

At the gate of patience
there is no crowding.

—MOROCCAN PROVERB

For everything there is a season, and a time for every matter under heaven: a time to be born, and a time to die; a time to plant, and a time to pluck up what is planted; a time to kill, and a time to heal; a time to break down, and a time to build up; a time to weep, and a time to laugh; a time to mourn, and a time to dance; a time to cast away stones,

and a time to gather stones together;
a time to embrace, and a time to
refrain from embracing; a time to
seek, and a time to lose; a time to
keep, and a time to cast away; a time
to rend, and a time to sew; a time to
keep silence, and a time to speak; a
time to love, and a time to hate; a
time for war, and a time for peace.

—ECCLESIASTES 3:1–8

Tranquillity! thou better name
Than all the family of Fame.

—SAMUEL TAYLOR COLERIDGE

$\mathscr{P}$ATIENCE is the one virtue whose lessons we cannot avoid.

Let nothing disturb thee,
Let nothing affright thee,
All things are passing,
God changeth never.

—HENRY WADSWORTH
LONGFELLOW

$\mathcal{P}$ATIENCE and anticipation may seem opposites, but in fact they can go hand-in-hand. Few of us live in the eternal present. We look forward to the events and seasons of our lives with eagerness or anxiety, and sometimes with both. Patience allows us to experience fully what is happening at the moment even as we keep an eye on the future. The patient person doesn't have to deny the here and now in order to live for tomorrow.

He that can have patience
can have what he will.

—Benjamin Franklin

Do not mistake patience for passivity. Patience fills us with an inner strength and a quiet, unassuming power. When we take the time to do things as we should, and to let nature take its course, then we allow ourselves, our actions, and our concerns the time to find their true meaning and form.

Grain by grain, a loaf—
stone by stone, a castle.

—Yugoslavian proverb

$\mathcal{P}$ATIENCE is a means as well as an end. As we strive to meet certain goals, or simply await certain events of our lives, our anxiety decreases as our patience increases. And the less anxiety we feel, the more likely we are to meet the challenges of everyday life with grace, imagination, and understanding.

Patience is the
companion of wisdom.
—ST. AUGUSTINE

No thing great is created
suddenly, any more than a bunch
of grapes or a fig. If you tell me
that you desire a fig, I answer you
that there must be time. Let it first
blossom, then bear fruit, then ripen.

—EPICTETUS

A patient man will control
himself for a while,
And afterward joy will break out.

—BEN SIRA

A NOISELESS PATIENT SPIDER

A noiseless patient spider,
I mark'd where on a little promontory
    it stood isolated,
Mark'd how to explore the vacant
    vast surrounding,
It launch'd forth filament, filament,
    filament, out of itself,
Ever unreeling them, ever tirelessly
    speeding them.

    —WALT WHITMAN

Long is not forever.
—GERMAN PROVERB

*T*HERE is no one so impatient as a child on Christmas Eve . . . unless you count the frustrated parents trying to put together the "easy-to-assemble" bicycle that Santa Claus dropped off. Holidays and special events often call for increased levels of patience. Try making these occasions your personal tests. You might be surprised—and gratified—with the results.

Be patient with everyone, but above all with thyself. I mean, do not be disheartened by your imperfections, but always rise up with fresh courage.

—ST. FRANCIS DE SALES

$\mathcal{M}$ONEY, when tended carefully, increases. Cheese, when left to age, improves. Allow matters sufficient time and you will be rewarded. Patience will eventually deliver what you want.

Victory is not won in miles
but in inches. Win a little
now, hold your ground, and
later win a little more.
—LOUIS L'AMOUR

My soul, sit thou a patient looker-on;
Judge not the play before the play
    is done:
Her plot hath many changes; every day
Speaks a new scene; the last act crowns
    the play.

—FRANCIS QUARLES

Patience and diligence, like
faith, remove mountains.
— WILLIAM PENN

Patience is the art of hoping.
— MARQUIS DE VAUVENARGUES

At the bottom of patience
one finds heaven.

—KANURI (WEST AFRICAN)

PROVERB

*D*o you love the autumn? If so, then summer's heat and sun-loving crowds are the ultimate test as you long for cool evenings and russet-colored leaves. Those same leaves, however, can try the patience of a skier who dreams of steep slopes covered with powdery snow. So it is for each of us: some seasons speed by too quickly, others endlessly linger, and none will hurry no matter how hard we urge.

This is where patience shows its ultimate value: it keeps us from wishing the
seasons of our lives away.

Every day a thread makes
a skein in a year.

—DUTCH PROVERB

Wait and see.

—HERBERT HENRY ASQUITH

The text of this book was set in
Centaur and the display in Zipper.

Book design and typesetting by
SARA E. STEMEN